WELLS CATHEDRAL

ABOVE: *A view of Wells Cathedral. It shows how the various parts mount pyramidally to the apex of the central tower.*

WELLS CATHEDRAL

The Very Reverend F. P. Harton B.D., Late Dean of Wells

THE Diocese of Bath and Wells, whose Cathedral this is, has seen over a thousand years of English history. Ancient Wessex extended from Surrey to Cornwall and was divided into two bishoprics, Winchester and Sherborne, but by the beginning of the 10th century it had become clear that this vast tract of difficult country was far too large to be administered effectively by only two bishops. Edward the Elder therefore took advantage of the death of both prelates within a year to carry out a much more practical plan of division by shires, assigning Wiltshire and Berkshire to the new see of Ramsbury, Devon and Cornwall to Crediton and Somerset to Wells, to which Athelm was consecrated in 909.

The diocese was then Wells, now it is Bath and Wells, a fact which frequently causes some perplexity, and we must enquire how this came about.

For close on two hundred years the Saxon bishops of Somerset were happily content to be bishops of Wells, but John de Villula, a Norman who became bishop in 1088, had other ideas. He had designs upon Bath and obtained both city and abbey from William Rufus. He then destroyed the canonical buildings at Wells, turning the canons out to live as best they could, and made himself Bishop of Bath only.

Bishop Robert of Lewes (1136–1166) was a very different person; though retaining the title of Bishop of Bath, he set himself to restore Wells to its rightful position and to recover it from the sad state in which he found it. Although allowing Bath

*

FACING PAGE: *Two aerial views of the cathedral. Top, from the south-west. Bottom, from the north.*

RIGHT: *The font. It may perhaps have survived from the earlier cathedral which lay to the south of the present building. The cover is Jacobean.*

to retain the precedence which it had acquired under John de Villula, he laid down that the bishop should have his throne in both Wells Cathedral and Bath Abbey, and that he should be elected by both Chapters conjointly.

A further complication however arose under Bishop Savaric (1192–1205). He was even more ambitious and unscrupulous than John de Villula. Disregarding the procedure laid down by Robert he managed by successful scheming to obtain the bishopric without reference to the Chapter of Wells. But neither Wells nor Bath satisfied him; the ancient abbey of Glastonbury was in his diocese and upon this he laid rapacious hands. Appointed abbot by Richard I, he obtained jurisdiction over the abbey and under John he took possession of it by violence. He then assumed the title of Bath and Glastonbury.

Jocelin succeeded as Bishop of Bath and Glastonbury in 1206 but in 1219 gave up the abbacy, reverting to the title of Bishop of Bath.

There was further trouble at the accession of Bishop Roger in 1244. Once again the monks of Bath made a bid to recover their supremacy and broke the agreement of Robert of Lewes, obtaining royal sanction and papal confirmation without consultation with the Chapter of Wells and before that body could make any move. This produced a spate of legislation, the upshot of which was that the Pope confirmed Roger's election but decreed that the agreement of Robert of Lewes should thenceforth be adhered to, the bishop using the title of Bath and Wells. Bishop Roger and all his successors have retained that title though it is no longer strictly applicable, for, since the dissolution of Bath Abbey in 1539, the bishop has been elected by the Chapter of Wells only and his throne remains in this Cathedral.

It will be remembered that at the coronation of Queen Elizabeth II the Bishop of Bath and Wells shared with the Bishop of Durham the privilege of supporting the Sovereign; this is interesting as showing the importance of tradition in national affairs. Bath and Wells is not one of the most important dioceses, and one might expect that it would have been the privilege of London or Winchester to support the Sovereign; that it is not is due simply to the fact that at the coronation of Richard I, Reginald de Bohun, Bishop of Bath, and Hugh Pudsey, Bishop of Durham, discharged that office and their successors have retained it ever since.

We have had occasion to mention two worldly and ambitious prelates but Wells has also had saintly bishops. William Bitton II (1267–74) was so

Continued on page 5

renowned for saintliness that when Robert Kilwardby (himself a man of holiness and learning) was elected Archbishop of Canterbury, he chose to receive consecration at his hands, while so great was the impression made by his holy life on the Somerset folk that after his death they venerated him as a saint. Pilgrimages were made to his tomb in the Cathedral and many miracles were wrought there, more particularly on those afflicted with dental troubles. William de Marchia (1293–1302) also had such a reputation for sanctity that two attempts were made to obtain his canonisation.

Perhaps the best known and certainly not the least holy of Somerset bishops was Thomas Ken and it is characteristic of Charles II that, when the see fell vacant by the translation of Peter Mews to Winchester, he insisted on bringing from Winchester to Wells "the little black fellow who refused his lodging to poor Nelly," and he it was who ministered to Charles on his death bed. At the Revolution he was deprived of his see as a non-juror. He is said to have composed his evening hymn "Glory to thee, my God, this night" on the terrace walk of the Palace at Wells, and one hopes this may be true. He died in 1710 and was buried at Frome.

The Cathedral Church of Saint Andrew in Wells is one of the most lovely of all the cathedrals of England; not only has it a delicate beauty all its own but it is unique in many ways—the west front, the carved capitals, the Chapter House stair, the Chain Gate, Vicars' Choral Hall, Vicars' Close are

Continued on page 6

*

FACING PAGE: *The nave. Although the nave is now used frequently for large County services, it was not originally intended for services, but only as a covered way for processions on great festivals such as Easter and Whitsunday. The painting on the vault, made in the nineteenth century, is said to be a copy of the original pattern found beneath the whitewash.*

RIGHT: *When the central tower was raised to its present height in 1315–1322, it started to tilt westwards. In 1338 cracks appeared in the masonry. The ingenious inverted arches, shown here, were inserted about 1340 to transfer the weight from west to east, to brace the supports of the tower and to widen the foundations.*

to be found nowhere else—while, as Professor Freeman once said, "there is no other place where you can see so many of the ancient buildings still standing and still put to their own use."

Tradition has it that about the year 705 King Ina, by the advice of Saint Aldhelm, Bishop of Sherborne, founded a church here in honour of Saint Andrew with a college of secular priests to serve it; and it is certainly true that, when the bishopric of Wells was founded in 909, this church became its Cathedral and these priests its canons. We may think of this first Cathedral as somewhat resembling the Saxon church at Bradford-on-Avon, but in course of time it fell into decay or possibly was largely destroyed by John de Villula and none of it now remains.

That Cathedral was enlarged by Bishop Robert of Lewes and consecrated in 1148. The font which we still use possibly belonged to it, but the building itself has vanished completely.

The Cathedral we now see was begun by Bishop Reginald de Bohun between 1175 and 1185 and his original plan was so carefully developed by later builders that the whole building forms a unity so harmonious that one is never brought up short by breaks in design or style although some two and a half centuries separate Reginald from Bubwith.

The stone of which the Cathedral was built was quarried at Doulting, a village some eight miles from Wells, and it is interesting to note that, when replacements have to be made today, the stone still comes from the same

Continued on page 8

*

LEFT: *This famous clock in the north transept was made about 1390. When the clock strikes, figures of armed horsemen rotate, and at each circuit one knight is beaten down. The clock has a 24-hour dial, with the larger star representing the sun as hour "hand"; and a smaller star in the next circle acts as the minute "hand". The third dial shows the day of the lunar month.*

FACING PAGE: *The beautiful St. Stephen's chapel was furnished by the Mothers' Union in Somerset to the designs of Sir Ninian Comper. The cresting of the screen on the right of the chapel is particularly interesting, and the east window, with its jumble of 14th-century glass, looks especially lovely in the early morning.*

quarry. It was at Doulting too that Saint Aldhelm died in 709.

Bishop Reginald built the three western bays of the quire, the transepts, the four eastern bays of the nave and the north porch and his work was continued by Bishop Jocelin de Welles. Jocelin and his brother Hugh (afterwards Bishop of Lincoln) were, as their name implies, natives of the city and possessors of considerable wealth which they gave generously to the completion and beautifying of the Cathedral they loved. Jocelin had been canon and Hugh archdeacon under Reginald and were clearly of one mind with him. Jocelin completed the nave and consecrated the church in 1239.

The quire at this time extended beneath the central tower and included the first bay of the nave, on the west side of which stood the rood screen, which continued across the aisles. There were as yet neither Chapter House nor library, the north transept being used for both purposes.

Jocelin died in 1242 while work was continuing on the West Front. In the time of Bishop Bitton the undercroft was added and the Chapter House stair built to the roof of the undercroft, the Chapter House itself being begun by Bishop William de Marchia (1293–1302) and completed by Dean John de Godelee (1306–33), who also raised

the central tower (1321) and added the Lady Chapel.

It must not be imagined that the Cathedral had to wait until the 14th century for a Lady Chapel. Bishop Savaric who, in spite of his many faults had some devotion, did in fact found a mass of Our Lady to be sung daily in her chapel. This was the *capella B.M.V. iuxta claustrum* and stood east of the cloister. The first chapel on this site was probably built by Bishop Giso (1060–88). This was enlarged as a sort of private chapel by the Bitton family after the death of Bishop Bitton I and a much larger chapel was built by Bishop Stillington (1466–91). For some two hundred years the Cathedral had two Lady Chapels but nothing now remains of that by the cloister, since in 1552 Bishop Barlow delivered it over to a certain Sir John Gates (subsequently deservedly beheaded) for destruction.

Bishop Ralph of Shrewsbury (1329–63), whose magnificent tomb may be seen in the north quire aisle, completed the quire by adding the three eastern bays forming the presbytery and joined Dean Godelee's Lady Chapel to the main building by means of the retroquire. In his time, too, there was very nearly a major catastrophe. Dean Godelee's considerable addition to the central tower had added so greatly to its weight that it

was in danger of collapse. The inverted arches, now such a striking feature of the Cathedral, were therefore built in on three sides, the quire screen giving the necessary support on the fourth side, and so the tower has remained secure to this day.

The main building was now at last complete but more remained to be done exteriorly. The west front, though probably towers were originally intended, had remained without them until Bishop Harewell (1366–1386) contributed two-thirds of the cost of building the south-west tower, and Bishop Bubwith who died in 1424 provided in his will for the north-west tower. The question is frequently asked, did the original design for these towers envisage spires? The answer to

Continued on page 10

★

ABOVE: *The eastern arm of the cathedral, showing the Lady Chapel, retroquire, south-east transept and presbytery. The Lady Chapel, built in the form of an irregular octagon, probably stood by itself for a short time and was subsequently joined to the rest of the cathedral.*

FACING PAGE: *The splendid vaulting of the retroquire with the Lady Chapel beyond. The north and south windows are 14th century glass and the east window is a 19th century restoration.*

this is no. There is no architectural provision for any additions and it is clear that spires on these towers would have dwarfed the central and most important tower, which no architect would have desired to do; moreover spires are not characteristic of Somerset.

A last addition was the rebuilding of the cloister, of which the east side with the library over was built by Bishop Bubwith's executors under his will, and the west side with quire school, singing room and audit room by Bishop Beckington in 1457.

One later addition remains to be mentioned. Hugh Sugar (†1489), whose chantry stands beneath, had placed a rood in the traditional place above the inverted arch. This was destroyed at the Reformation but the sockets remained and in 1920 under Dean Armitage Robinson the present rood was placed in the same sockets, thus restoring the original intention and providing a valuable aid to devotion to worshippers in the nave.

So through the ages the Cathedral has grown. Built for the glory of God by successive generations of devoted men, this is no cold museum of antique exhibits, however lovely, but a holy place, living and warm with a thousand years of prayer, in which day by day, the worship of the faithful ascends to the Most High, a place of pilgrimage rather than sight-seeing, wherein in our own troubled age, men and women and children find peace and strength in the eternal.

*   *   *

The body known today as the Dean and Chapter has a continuous history of over 1,200 years, beginning with the college of priests established here by Saint Aldhelm in 705. Of them we know nothing beyond the fact that they were a missionary body, set in the midst of difficult country to maintain the worship of God and convert the heathen Saxons. They were not monks (Wells has never been monastic) but they must have led a common life of some sort. They had a church but how or where they lived we know not.

On the foundation of the diocese in 909 their church became the Cathedral and they themselves the first canons, clergy of the bishop's *familia* appointed by him to serve the Cathedral.

The early bishops had their hands full with missionary labours and the building up of the new diocese, with the result that the canons, while faithfully maintaining the worship of God, were seriously neglected, so that when Giso became bishop in 1061 he found but four or five canons here, living in miserable poverty supported by the alms of the faithful.

On the Continent, where similar conditions prevailed, it was being discovered that the old method of

Continued on page 14

*

ABOVE: *The beautiful needlework which adorns the stalls was begun in 1937 and completed in 1948. The banners in the back stalls bear the arms of bishops.*

FACING PAGE: *This is the centre of the cathedral's life, for here the worship of God goes on day by day as it has for over seven hundred years. Bishop Reginald's quire ends where the pulpit now stands and Bishop Ralph's continues eastwards. On the right is the Bishop's Throne with the Beckington Chantry beyond. The east window, known as the "Golden Window", is a most magnificent achievement in glass and was inserted in 1340. The figures below the window, representing Our Lord, with Saints Andrew and Peter, Dunstan, Patrick, David and George, were inserted as memorials after World War I.*

staffing cathedrals was highly unsatisfactory and a more worthy and orderly way of life was being evolved, notably by Saint Chrodegang at Metz. Giso, himself a Lorrainer, brought the new ideas with him and speedily reorganised his Cathedral. He gave his canons a regular community life under the rule of Saint Chrodegang and built them a cloister, refectory and dormitory, wherein to live together.

This happy state of affairs came to an end in 1088 when John de Villula destroyed the canonical buildings and the canons found themselves living as best they might among the towns folk.

Robert of Lewes (1135) set himself to recover Wells from its humiliation under John and made it once more a Cathedral. Applying the principles of the Norman bishops he established a Chapter of fifty canons, of whom five

were dignitaries (the *Quinque Personae*); the Dean to preside over the Chapter, the Precentor to rule the quire, the Chancellor, who had charge of the books, muniments and school, the Treasurer, who was responsible for the ornaments and treasures of the Cathedral, together with the Archdeacon of Wells, representing the Bishop; there were also two lesser dignitaries to assist the Dean and the Precentor, the Sub-Dean and the Succentor. Of this body two canonries were subsequently suppressed with the office of the Succentor, but the remainder are still in existence together with the five *Personae*, and the Sub-Dean.

To support this large body Bishop Robert greatly increased the endowments of the Cathedral, assigning to each canonry an estate or part of an estate (Combe supported fifteen canons) to provide his living. The technical name for these estates was "prebends" (a word derived from the same root as "provender"): the canons were therefore prebendaries. Although their estates have long since passed from the Cathedral to the Church Commissioners, each prebendary still retains his ancient title, which may be seen above his stall in the Chapter House.

The constitution of Bishop Robert has remained substantially in being to the present day but certain changes took place in the upheaval of the Reformation. In 1547 Dean Fitzwilliam was induced to surrender his deanery to Edward VI by whom it was recreated by private act of Parliament and conferred upon one John Goodman by letter patent. This action created a serious situation for, under the constitution, the Dean had always been elected by the Chapter and the canons refused then to accept the royal appointment; moreover the ancient Dean and Chapter were a body

Continued on page 16

★

LEFT: *The 13th-century stairway leading to the chapter house was extended to the Chain Bridge in the middle of the 15th century.*

FACING PAGE: *The chapter house, probably completed by 1306, gives a great sense of light, space and air. Here the Greater Chapter meets, each member in his own stall marked with the name of his office or the place of his prebend.*

corporate and the question inevitably arose as to what was the relation of the royally appointed Dean to the elected Chapter. To resolve these difficulties Dean Herbert and the Chapter petitioned the Crown for a Charter which was granted by Queen Elizabeth I in 1592. By this it was established that the existing Dean and Chapter were in fact identical with the ancient one, the ancient rights and customs remaining in full vigour. For the more practical administration of the Cathedral however the Chapter itself was divided into two parts, the management of the Cathedral being placed in the hands of the Dean with a Chapter of eight residentiary canons including the dignitaries, while the remaining, mainly non-resident, canons who henceforward dropped the title of canon, retaining that of prebendary, were left with their dignity but few responsibilities, forming with the residentiaries a single body called the Greater Chapter.

Under the Cathedral Act of 1855 the number of residentiary canons was reduced to four, no longer to be elected by the Dean and Chapter itself but appointed by the Bishop. Under the same Act the valuable estates belonging to the Chapter were alienated to the body now called the Church Commissioners from whom the Dean and Chapter received, and still do receive, a relatively small annuity and are consequently very largely dependent upon the alms of visitors for the upkeep of the Cathedral which has been their care through the centuries.

*   *   *

After the Cathedral itself some of the most striking buildings in Wells are the Chain Gate and Vicars' Close with its hall and chapel and to understand the reason of their existence one needs to become acquainted with another Cathedral body—that of the Vicars Choral.

As has been seen, the Chapter as constituted by Bishop Robert consisted of fifty canon prebendaries—a very large number, not all of whom were always present in quire, some of whom were not even resident in Wells, but all of whom were necessary to the due performance of the Cathedral worship; for which reason the canons had to provide substitutes when they were unable for any cause to carry out their quire duties. Hence there grew up a body of vicars, or canonical deputies, appointed by the canons, subject to the approval of the Dean and under the authority of the Dean and Chapter, and holding their stalls in quire immediately below those of the canons, real though subordinate members of the Cathedral body. All vicars were required to be in quire daily for the capitular mass and mass of Our Lady and the greater hours, six a side being a minimum required for the lesser hours.

Continued on page 18

*

LEFT: *The east cloister, built with a legacy from Nicholas Bubwith, Bishop 1407–1424. The library is above. The monuments were placed here on their removal from the Lady Chapel and nave during the restoration of 1842–1844.*

FACING PAGE: *The library built over the east cloister. It suffered greatly under the Commonwealth. The present panelling and bookcases, one of which with contemporary books and chains is shown below, were installed in 1685. The Hayles Psalter, (below left), a most beautiful manuscript, was written by a famous one-eyed scribe from Bois-le-Duc for the Monastery of Hayles in Gloucestershire and presented to the cathedral about a century ago.*

Liber Monasterii de Hayles

During the 12th and 13th centuries the vicars had no real common life but lodged either with their masters or by twos in the city, a most unsatisfactory state of affairs which led to much trouble and in 1318 the Dean and Chapter began to think about providing a common residence; they did indeed mark out a house but nothing further was done about it.

A new era, however, began in 1348 when the existing untidy arrangement was ended by Bishop Ralph of Shrews-bury and the vicars were constituted a corporate body with their own statutes and common seal as the College of Vicars Choral.

Bishop Ralph gave the vicars not only a constitution but a common life. No longer had they to lodge promiscuously in the city but he built each of them his own house and Vicars' Close remains as the monument of his care and generosity. Further he gave them within the Close a hall in which they dined, with its exchequer and muniment room, and a chapel in which to pray and say mass, both of which are still to be seen.

Previously the vicars had been paid, somewhat exiguously one fears, by their masters, though Bishop Jocelin, recognising them as part of the Cathedral foundation, granted them in addition a quotidian of a penny a day from the common fund of the Cathedral, but under Bishop Ralph they acquired their own estates and properties and so became self-supporting. For all these things the Vicars Choral have remembered Bishop Ralph with veneration and gratitude. His good work was continued by Bishop Beckington, that great builder. He revised the Vicars' statutes, built the library over the Close Chapel and the Chain Gate connecting the Vicars' Hall with the Chapter House and the Cathedral, the purpose of which was to provide the vicars with a covered way by which, particularly at night and in inclement weather, they could pass from their hall to the Cathedral without leaving their own territory.

Bishop Beckington's executors made some improvements in the Close which are now hard to identify, as also did Bishop Bubwith (1407–25).

The College of Vicars continued to flourish until the Reformation brought changes. Fortunately for them they were not part of a monastic foundation nor were they chantry priests, so they escaped the fate of the religious houses and of their brethren the Annuellars in the Mounterey, nevertheless "severall doubts and questions were had and made of concerning the validitie of this body politick or Corporation of these Vicars Chorall," so they, like the Dean and Chapter, obtained a new Charter from Queen Elizabeth I, which may still be seen, along with

Continued on page 22

★

LEFT: *One of the windows of the Lady Chapel. These windows of 14th-century glass were either deliberately smashed or allowed to disintegrate because no one was willing to have them repaired. They were patched with glass from other windows, partly at the restoration of 1660 onwards and again in the nineteenth century.*

FACING PAGE: Vicars' *Hall or refectory was built in or before 1348 by Bishop Ralph of Shrewsbury, who referred then to "the buildings I have built and shall build" for the College of Vicars Choral.*

other documents, in the Vicars' Hall.

A great, though inevitable change occurred at this time to the vicars themselves. Before the Reformation, although they might join the college as laymen under probation, they had to be at least in minor orders thereafter, but when minor orders were extinguished the situation altered radically. It was still necessary for some of the vicars to be in priest's orders but the greater part of them were then required only as singing men and so could be, and in fact were, laymen. They still, however, remained vicars, unlike the singing men and minor canons of the cathedrals of the new foundation. So came about the distinction which is still maintained between lay and priest vicars.

Under the Commonwealth the Vicars Choral, like the Dean and Chapter themselves, were extinguished and "did extreamly suffer, and were turned out of doores, plundered, and imprisoned," but at the Restoration they, with the Dean and Chapter, returned to enjoy their own again.

This they continued to do until the passing of the Cathedrals Measure in 1931 which dissolved all minor corporate bodies in cathedral churches. By this measure their corporate rights and freeholds were dissolved and their chapel, hall and other possessions were transferred to the Dean and Chapter "in particular for the use and benefit of the Vicars," their houses passing to the Church Commissioners, though they themselves remained the College of Vicars of the Cathedral Church of St. Andrew in Wells, their number being fixed at not fewer than nine lay vicars and not less than two priest vicars.

*   *   *

Wells Cathedral School is the oldest educational foundation in Somerset. The Mayor and Corporation of Wells in 1880 claimed that it began with the see in 909 and they were probably right. However that may be, it was certainly in existence before 1140 under the control of the Chancellor.

It is probable that in the early period scholars were taught in the Cathedral itself and boarded out with Vicars Choral and others in the city, but early in the 13th century the school acquired a new habitation when a certain Roger de Chyuton, chaplain to the Bishop and Canon of the Cathedral granted his houses to the cathedral for the use of the school. The grant was confirmed in perpetuity by Archbishop Peckham in 1281. This house was in the Mounterey, now called the Liberty.

At the end of the 14th century the College of Annuellars or Chantry Priests was established in the Mounterey which before long took over the

Continued on page 24

*

ABOVE: *The "New Works", then Penniless Porch, leading to the cathedral, where beggars used to sit and solicit alms; and the Bishop's Eye, leading to the Bishop's Palace, all built by Bishop Beckington.*

FACING PAGE: *The wall and moat surrounding the Palace were constructed by Bishop Ralph in 1340. At the left of the Gatehouse the swans gather at the sound of the bell, and then pull the bell-rope when they wish to be fed.*

school house, the school moving temporarily to "a house in Torre Lane by the Torregate," afterwards returning to the Mounterey to an outhouse on the messuage of Canon Thomas Frome, which was later enlarged for their use. About 1465 the school moved to rooms over the newly built west cloister, where it remained until 1870.

In 1547 the Commissioners under the Chantries Act reported that "the Dean and Chapter of Wells of their frewill keepe and mayntayne a free Grammar Scole there and do pay to the Master of the said scole yerely for his stipend or wages £13 6s. 8d. and to the usher of the said scole yerely £6 13s. 4d." By that time the "scole" was served by an usher as well as a master.

The school continued its existence throughout the changes of Henry VIII, Edward VI and Mary I and in 1592 Queen Elizabeth I granted a Charter to the Dean and Chapter which mentions the schoolmaster as one of the ministers of the Cathedral church and

*

ordains that the same payments as have been made during the preceding twenty years should be paid to him.

Another feature of the Elizabethan Charter is the union of the Singing School with the Grammar School. The Singing School was of equal age with the Grammar School but had always existed as a separate entity governed by the Master of the Quiristers under the Precentor; its object was the training of the quiristers in music and rendering of divine worship. The union of 1592 is still operative, the Cathedral quiristers being educated in the Grammar School and trained for their singing duties by the Master of the Quiristers.

Under the Commonwealth the Dean and Chapter were deprived of their offices and emoluments, as were all members of the Cathedral establishment with the single exception of the schoolmaster, one Robert Aysh who, appointed in 1622, retained his office until his death in 1657. "One Sampson" was then appointed, who is described as "very unable, cannot give account of his grammer . . . hath spoiled the school." Nevertheless the school continued without break until the appointment of John Oker at the Restoration. After that it continued with varying fortunes. Henry Mills (1710–17) was said to have "in a few years raised the reputation of this school far above what former masters

could effect in many years." On the other hand its headmaster John Vickery was made headmaster of the Blue School, then occupying St. Andrew's Lodge in the Liberty, which had been built as the Charity School. He took with him a number of boarders from the Cathedral School, when the Blue School moved in 1829. Nevertheless, in 1833 the Cathedral School was still in existence with 26 boys.

In 1876 the school suffered a temporary eclipse. Its numbers were down to three and the aged schoolmaster retired. The greater part of their endowments having been sequestrated to the Ecclesiastical Commissioners, the Dean and Chapter were in no position to maintain the school; the quiristers were therefore sent to a private school in Chamberlain Street, kept by Mr. J. Palmer, and the Cathedral School was suspended until the Dean and Chapter should be in a position to re-establish it.

In 1881 it was in fact re-established and in 1884 fully reconstituted in a building in the Liberty built and given by Canon Bernard. Since then it has grown to be a school of some 400 pupils including over 100 in the Junior School. It now occupies all the large buildings in the Liberty practically on the site of its original 13th-century home. In 1969 a large and fully equipped Sports Hall was completed and formally opened by H.M. Queen Elizabeth the Queen Mother. The Ritchie Hall, part of the Bernard Buildings and incorporating part of the Canons' Barn built in about 1190, was converted into a small Theatre and Concert Hall. In the same year the School began accepting girls as well as boys. The school continues to give special emphasis to the development of musical talent, not only among the quiristers but in all its pupils with musical ability.

So today this thousand-year-old school is in full vigour, giving not only a sound secular education but also, what is even more precious, a Christian education within the family of one of the most beautiful cathedrals of England.

*   *   *

ACKNOWLEDGMENTS

The photographs in this book are by Peter Baker, A.I.I.P., A.R.P.S., A. F. Kersting, A.I.I.P., F.R.P.S. and Aerofilms Ltd.

SBN 85372 077 0   272/50